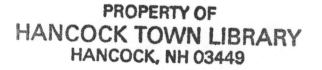

14637

African-American
Soldiers

Civil War Soldiers

Catherine Reef

Twenty-First Century Books

A Division of Henry Holt and Company
New York

PHOTO CREDITS

cover: flag by Fred J. Eckert/FPG International; photo courtesy of the National Archives. **3:** Bettmann. **4, 7, 10:** Schomburg Center for Research in Black Culture. **14:** Library of Congress. **17:** Massachusetts Commandery, Military Order of the Loyal Legion and the US Army Military History Institute. **20:** Library of Congress. **22:** Library of Congress. **26:** National Archives. **29:** Library of Congress. **30, 33:** National Archives. **35:** Library of Congress. **37:** Bettmann. **40, 41:** Massachusetts Commandery, Military Order of the Loyal Legion and the US Army Military History Institute. **42:** Schomburg Center for Research in Black Culture. **45:** Library of Congress. **46:** Massachusetts Historical Society. **49:** Massachusetts Commandery, Military Order of the Loyal Legion and the US Army Military History Institute. **51:** Library of Congress. **53:** Massachusetts Historical Society. **56:** National Archives. **61:** Schomburg Center for Research in Black Culture. **65, 68:** Bettmann. **75:** Bettmann.

Twenty-First Century Books
A Division of Henry Holt and Company, Inc.
115 West 18th Street
New York, NY 10011

Henry Holt® and colophon are registered trademarks of
Henry Holt and Company, Inc.
Publishers since 1866.

Text Copyright © 1993 by Catherine Reef
All rights reserved.
Published in Canada by Fitzhenry & Whiteside Ltd.,
91 Granton Drive, Richmond Hill, Ontario L4B 2N5

Library of Congress Cataloging-in-Publication Data

Reef, Catherine
Civil War soldiers / Catherine Reef. — 1st ed.
p. cm. — (African-American soldiers)
Includes biographical references and index.
Summary: Describes the crucial role played by African-American soldiers
in securing victory for the Union in the Civil War.
1. United States—History—Civil War, 1861-1865—Participation,
Afro-American—Juvenile literature. 2. Afro-American
soldiers—History—19th century—Juvenile literature.
[1. United States—History—Civil War, 1861-1865—Participation,
Afro-American. 2. Afro-American soldiers—History—19th century.]
I. Title. II. Series.
E540.N3R44 1993
973.7'415—dc20 92-34412 CIP AC

ISBN 0-8050-2371-2
First Edition—1993

Printed in Mexico
All first editions are printed on acid-free paper ∞.

10 9 8 7 6 5 4 3 2 1

Contents

Chapter 1

No Braver Company

Sunrise was several hours away, but already the air was hot and muggy. The waters of the Mississippi River flowed quietly around the curve called Milliken's Bend.

In the early morning of June 7, 1863, Union soldiers waited in the Louisiana darkness. They listened for the rustle of movement through the trees—a warning that the Confederate Army was approaching. They listened for the "rebel yell," the enemy's spine-chilling battle cry.

Union and Confederate, North and South— only a few years earlier, the soldiers who faced one another at Milliken's Bend had been fellow countrymen. Now they were deep in a bloody civil war. The soldiers of the southern states—the Confederate States of America—fought for independence and the right to decide the future of southern

An unidentified Civil War soldier poses proudly.

slavery. The Union soldiers fought to unite their divided country and free the four million slaves of the south.

The soldiers camped along the Mississippi in those pre-dawn hours would soon experience war firsthand. Sweat poured from their faces. They grew more uneasy as the minutes passed. In the Union camp at Milliken's Bend, there was an added reason for concern. The African-American soldiers who waited in the darkness, two regiments of raw recruits, had never fought a battle. Some had spent only two days learning how to fire their old muskets and use their bayonets. The white soldiers wondered about these newly armed black men. Did they have the courage to fight? Would they turn and run from battle?

The Confederates attacked in the early morning hours, and the African-American soldiers faced them bravely. They proved that they possessed the same courage and ability as white troops.

This was not the first war in which African Americans fought for their country. Twice before—in the American Revolution and the War of 1812—black soldiers had answered the call to arms. After each war, however, their service and sacrifice were forgotten. The U.S. armed forces rejected African

Americans when the threat of war was over.

The sun rose over the southern landscape, and soon the temperature neared one hundred degrees. The Confederates pushed the Union troops back toward the river. Cornered and outnumbered, the

African-American soldiers faced the test of battle at Milliken's Bend.

black soldiers refused to surrender. They battled on through the morning in hand-to-hand combat. They fought with their bayonets and wooden rifle butts. "It was a horrible fight, the worst I was ever engaged in," observed Captain M. M. Miller, a white officer.

The African Americans who fought at Milliken's Bend were ordinary men. Many of them had been slaves themselves, and their hatred of slavery fueled their courage. "Before I would be a slave again," said a soldier from Louisiana, "I would fight till the last drop of blood was gone."

One black soldier, a man nicknamed "Big Jack" Jackson, struck down so many Confederates that he shattered his rifle butt. Bleeding from bayonet wounds, Jackson fought on through the morning. He kept on fighting until a Confederate bullet took his life. Another African-American soldier, whose name is now forgotten, had his jaw broken in the battle. In raging pain, he stayed at his post until his commander ordered him to the rear. "I never saw a braver company of men in my life," noted Captain Miller.

At midday, two Union gunboats came into view. The cannons protruding from the armored ships fired a single volley, and the Confederates decided to retreat. The Union Army had won the Battle of Milliken's Bend.

The cost of victory was high. Dead and wounded men lay everywhere. A third of the black soldiers had been killed or injured. The Southern troops captured fifty black soldiers, along with two of their white officers. They sold some of the captured black soldiers as slaves and murdered others, according to some reports.

"They met death coolly, bravely," Miller said of his black troops. He walked among the trees and on the riverbank, where the dead had fallen. "I never felt more grieved and sick at heart," Miller wrote, "than when I saw how my brave soldiers had been slaughtered."

Though poorly trained and poorly equipped, these black recruits had held their ground. Their commanding general spoke with admiration when he noted that "it is impossible for men to show greater bravery than the Negro troops in that fight." One of the white officers remarked, "There is no better material for soldiers than they."

African-American soldiers helped the Union win an important victory at Milliken's Bend. Taking part in more than four hundred Civil War battles, they went on to help the Union win the

"It is impossible for men to show greater bravery than the Negro troops in that fight."

war. At the end of the war, Dr. Martin Delany, the Army's first black major, addressed a group of former slaves. "If it was not for the black man," Delany said, "this war would never have been brought to a close with success to the Union and the liberty of your race."

But black soldiers also fought battles within

Dr. Martin Delany

the Union Army. They fought to receive the same treatment as white soldiers. They fought to gain the respect of their fellow Americans.

These battles did not end in 1865, when the Union won the Civil War. African Americans in the U.S. military have continued to fight against prejudice. They have continued the struggle for equal opportunity. It was only after the Civil War, for instance, that the U.S. Army accepted African Americans during peacetime. It was not until 1940 that an African American became a general in the active regular Army. It was not until 1948 that black and white soldiers worked side by side in an integrated Army. And it was not until 1989 that an African-American soldier served as chairman of the Joint Chiefs of Staff, the group of high-ranking officers responsible for America's military operations.

That chairman, General Colin Powell, takes pride in the African-American tradition of service. "I will never forget the courage and the determination of African Americans who defied all odds to fight for their country," he has said, "African Americans who wore the uniform of the U.S. Army as proudly and courageously as any other American who ever wore it."

Chapter 2

The Sleeping Serpent

Fort Sumter stood on a tiny island in the harbor of Charleston, South Carolina. With cannons at the top of its brick walls, the American military base stood ready to fight off attacks by foreign navies. But when Fort Sumter came under attack in 1861, the assault was from land, and the enemy was from home.

At 4:30 AM, on April 12, 1861, the dark sky above Charleston's harbor grew bright with gunfire. Again and again, the soldiers of the Confederacy aimed their cannons at the fort and fired.

Major Robert Anderson and sixty-eight soldiers of the U.S. Army fought back as well as they could. But they could not stop the cannon balls that made craters in the walls of the fort; they could not stop the exploding mortar shells that set many wooden structures on fire. "We came very near being stifled with the dense living smoke from the burning buildings," one officer reported.

The Union soldiers surrendered Fort Sumter after thirty-three hours of battle. On April 14, the Confederate flag flew over the fort. "Our Southern brethren have done grievous wrong," Anderson wrote. The attack on Fort Sumter marked the beginning of the American Civil War.

The roar of cannons had awakened the people of Charleston. Mary Chesnut, the wife of a former U.S. senator, was staying at a Charleston hotel. "There was a sound of stir all over the house, pattering of feet in the corridor," she wrote in her journal.

Chesnut sipped tea as she watched the siege of Fort Sumter. She also watched the African-American slaves who served her, and wondered what they thought of the attack. Did they foresee that this war would lead to the end of slavery? Neither the slaves' words nor their expressions gave away their feelings. The slaves appeared "silent and strong, biding their time," Chesnut wrote. She wondered whether they were wiser than their white masters.

Black Americans did find hope in the war, and not all of them were silent. "What a change now greets us!" wrote Frederick Douglass, editor of the abolitionist, or anti-slavery, newspaper, the *North Star*. Douglass, himself an escaped slave, was known for his anti-slavery speeches and writings. "The war now being waged in this land," he declared, "is a war for and against slavery."

Frederick Douglass

Blacks had been serving whites in North America since 1619, when the first African people were brought to the English colony of Virginia. The first blacks who landed at Jamestown in 1619 worked as servants, not as slaves. After a period of service, they received their freedom. But in the 1640s, white Virginians began to consider their black servants as "chattel slaves." In other words, they looked upon black workers as the personal property of their employers.

Colonial planters depended on slaves to plant and harvest their crops of tobacco, rice, and sugar cane. As more white settlers cleared land for farming, the demand for slave labor increased. Slaves had no rights whatsoever. Strict codes governed every aspect of their lives. As property, slaves were bought and sold at slave markets. Their children were born into slavery, and their families were broken up.

Many Americans disapproved of slavery. In the 1780s, several northern states—Pennsylvania, Massachusetts, Connecticut, Rhode Island, New York, and New Jersey—outlawed the practice of owning slaves. Thomas Jefferson and George Washington, slave owners themselves, thought that slavery would slowly die out. "Nothing is more certainly written in the book of fate," stated Jefferson, "than that these people are to be free."

Freedom for America's slaves was not to come quickly or easily. In 1789, the Constitution of the United States promised to "secure the Blessings of Liberty" for Americans. But those blessings were not secured for the 700,000 African Americans who lived as slaves. In fact, according to the Constitution, a slave was to be counted as only three-fifths of a free person when totaling a state's population. He or she had no right to freedom. In 1793, the U.S. Congress passed the first fugitive slave law, which allowed slave owners to recapture slaves who had escaped to free states.

Slavery did not die out, as Jefferson had hoped it would. In the 1800s, it grew more widespread. With the invention of the cotton gin in 1793, cotton became a very profitable crop to grow. The southern wilderness gave way to thousands of cotton plantations, each needing a steady supply of manual labor. By 1860, the slave population of the United States reached four million. One out of every seven Americans was a slave.

For most slaves, home was a windowless one-room shack with a dirt floor. Slaves slept on beds made of corn husks, blankets, or straw. They survived on a diet of cornmeal, salt pork, and molasses. Most slaves worked on farms, laboring in the fields from dawn until darkness. During the Louisiana sugar-cane harvest, many worked eighteen to twenty hours a day. If they did not work hard or fast enough, slaves often received whippings. "We were no more than dogs," declared one slave. Some planters worked their slaves to death. They figured it was cheaper to buy a new slave than to keep an old one alive.

By 1860, one out of every seven Americans was a slave.

While the southern economy depended on slaves, many Northerners claimed that slavery was wrong. But people tended to push the problem of slavery from their minds. The problem was, in the words of the American writer John Jay Chapman, "a sleeping serpent." As long as the problem lay quiet and out of sight, he explained, people could easily ignore it. But one day the serpent would wake up, Chapman warned.

The growth of America awakened the nation to the problem of slavery. The 1800s saw a great movement westward, as Americans settled the new states and territories beyond the Mississippi River. Southerners wanted to bring slavery into the newly settled lands, but many people in the north refused to accept the idea that slavery would spread as the country grew. One compromise followed another, as Americans tried to reach some form of agreement on the question of slavery.

The Missouri Compromise of 1820 allowed Missouri to enter the Union as a slave state while Maine entered as a free state, one where slavery was outlawed. The Missouri Compromise also drew an imaginary line running across the American West. Any new states located north of that line were to be free; any new states to the south of that line would be slave states.

But the slave question would not go away. Thirty years later, the nation needed another compromise to keep the peace. According to the Compromise of 1850, California became a new free state, while the future of slavery in the territories of New Mexico and Utah was left undecided. To please the South, Congress passed a new and stricter fugitive slave law. The lawmakers imposed a severe penalty for anyone who helped a runaway slave.

Both Southerners and Northerners reacted angrily to the new compromise. Anti-slavery leaders denounced the fugitive slave law. "Let the President drench our land of freedom in blood, but he will never make us obey *that* law," exclaimed Congressman Joshua Giddings of Ohio. Slavery's supporters believed the compromises took away a right guaranteed by the Constitution—the right of states to decide about slavery for themselves. To John C. Calhoun, a senator from South Carolina and former Vice President of the United States, the Compromise of 1850 was the beginning of the end of the Union. If the North insisted on limiting slavery, Calhoun argued, "tell us so and let the states we represent part in peace. If you are unwilling we should part in peace, tell us so, and we shall know what to do."

In 1850, some people still hoped that the Union could be preserved. Senator Daniel Webster of Massachusetts urged agreement "not as a Northern man, but as an American." But with each compromise on the slavery question, people on both sides grew angrier; on both sides, positions hardened. The country drifted toward war. Compromises could only postpone the coming storm.

Northern abolitionists wanted to do more than stop the spread of slavery—they wanted to abolish slavery altogether. "Urge me not to use moderation in a cause like the present," declared William Lloyd Garrison, publisher of the abolitionist newspaper *The Liberator*. "I will not retreat a single inch."

The masthead for the abolitionist newspaper, *The Liberator*

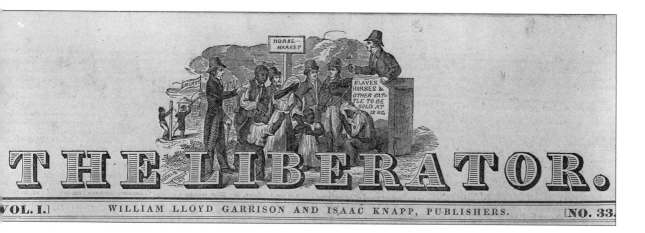

Soon after the Compromise of 1850 was passed, Harriet Beecher Stowe sat down to write *Uncle Tom's Cabin*. Her novel described the horrors of slavery. "I don't go for savin' niggers," says one character in the book, slave master Simon Legree. "Use up, and buy more, 's my way—makes you less trouble, and I'm quite sure it comes cheaper in the end." Within a year, more than 300,000 copies of *Uncle Tom's Cabin* were sold. Stowe's book became an American classic. Even today, many people read this important work.

Some abolitionists wanted to end slavery by force. In 1838, in a crowded Ohio church, a man with fiery eyes had stood up to announce, "Here, before God, I consecrate my life to the destruction of slavery." To some people, John Brown was a madman bent on violence; others hailed him as a hero, a courageous leader in the fight against slavery. In 1859, Brown and his band of followers attacked a government arsenal, a place for storing weapons, in Harpers Ferry, Virginia. Brown hoped that his actions would lead to a general slave revolt. Instead, the Army captured Brown and hung him for the crime of treason.

The Supreme Court fanned the angry flames in 1857 with its decision in the Dred Scott case.

Scott was a Missouri slave who had been brought to Illinois and the Minnesota Territory, where slavery was outlawed. Back in Missouri, Scott sued his owner, claiming that the time he had spent in Minnesota had made him free. The Supreme Court ruled that, because slaves were not citizens, Scott had no right to bring suit. Slaves were property, argued Chief Justice Roger B. Taney, and their owners were free to take them anywhere they liked.

Dred Scott

In 1860, with their nation nearly torn apart by the slavery dispute, Americans were going to vote for a new President. The Republican Party, formed from several groups opposed to the spread of slavery, nominated tall, lanky Abraham Lincoln of Illinois. Lincoln could see that the nation was heading toward war. "A house divided against itself cannot stand," Lincoln had declared in 1858. "I believe this government cannot endure, permanently, half slave and half free."

But Lincoln had no plans to end slavery. Like Thomas Jefferson, he hoped the practice would die "a natural death." Lincoln desired, above all, to keep the country united, even if the practice of slavery continued in the southern states.

Still, people in the south reacted to his election with alarm. In December 1860, South Carolina became the first southern state to secede, or withdraw, from the United States. By the time Lincoln moved into the White House, in March 1861, six other states—Mississippi, Florida, Alabama, Georgia, Louisiana, and Texas—had joined South Carolina in secession. Within weeks, Virginia, Arkansas, Tennessee, and North Carolina seceded as well. These eleven states formed a new nation, the Confederate States of America.

President Lincoln spoke to the Confederates when he made his first speech as president. "We must not be enemies," he said. "In your hands, my dissatisfied countrymen, and not mine is the momentous issue of civil war."

Lincoln wanted to reunite his nation without starting a war. But the Confederate states contained land and buildings that belonged to the U.S. government. One of these was Fort Sumter. The Union soldiers who were stationed there needed food and supplies. Having to resupply the fort, Lincoln assured the governor of South Carolina that he would not send weapons or more soldiers—as long as the fort was not attacked.

The Confederates did attack, however. And as the Charleston sky lit up with gunfire, the states of the north and south plunged into war.

Chapter 3

The White Man's War

After the attack on Fort Sumter, a wave of patriotism swept through African-American communities in the north. "Friends of freedom, be up and doing," cried Frederick Douglass. "Now is your time. Now is the day, and now is the hour."

Black men by the thousands offered to join the Union Army. "There was not a man who would not leap for his knapsack and musket," reported an African-American resident of Boston.

African Americans had good reasons to fight. Like white Northerners, they wanted to reunite their nation. Unlike most whites, however, they also wanted to wage war against slavery. At the time the Civil War began, the majority of whites were neither ready nor willing to fight to free the slaves. In fact, slavery was still legal in the four Union states known as the border states—Delaware, Maryland, Kentucky, and Missouri. It was even allowed in the nation's capital, Washington, D.C.

But soon after the start of the war, blacks learned they would be denied the right to serve their country. "This is a white man's war," people told them.

"Why does the government reject the negro?" Frederick Douglass wanted to know. "Is he not a man? Can he not wield a sword, fire a gun, march and countermarch, and obey orders like any other?"

At the time, there seemed to be no need for black recruits. With war fever running high, more than enough whites had volunteered to meet the demands of the Union Army. "Everyone seems willing to do everything and sacrifice everything for a common cause," said Carl Schurz, a well-known public speaker. Most people, on both sides, thought that the war would be a quick and easy one.

The Civil War began as a "white man's war" for another reason as well. Many whites doubted that African Americans would make good soldiers. General William T. Sherman expressed this common point of view: "Can a negro do our skirmishing and picket duty?" he asked. "Can they improvise bridges, sorties, flank movements, etc.,

General William T. Sherman

like the white man? I say no."

Like Sherman, most whites ignored or failed to remember the contributions made by African Americans in earlier wars. "They were good enough to help win American independence," Douglass said of America's black soldiers, "but they are not good enough to help preserve that independence against treason and rebellion."

By the time of the Civil War, African Americans had established a tradition of military service and heroism. That tradition began even before Americans declared their independence from England. In Boston, on the night of March 5, 1770, Crispus Attucks, a runaway slave, led a mob of people angry at the sight of British soldiers in their city. "The way to get rid of these soldiers," the colonists shouted, "is to attack their main guard!" Before Attucks's group set upon the soldiers, however, the British fired into the crowd. Attucks was the first to die.

It seemed wrong to many blacks that whites were demanding independence from England while continuing to own slaves. Still, 7,000 African Americans fought in the American Revolution. Because military leaders considered them unfit to command troops, blacks fought under white officers. They took part in every major battle of the war.

Among the Americans who fought at the Battle of Rhode Island on August 29, 1778, was a company of black soldiers. Led by a white officer, Colonel Christopher Greene, these African-American soldiers fought against Hessian troops. (The Hessians were German soldiers who had been hired by the British.) The Hessians singled out the black company for their heaviest attack. They expected the African-American soldiers to be poorly trained. Yet the black troops withstood three Hessian attacks and helped to win the battle. One of the German soldiers reported that America's black soldiers were "able-bodied, strong and brave fellows."

During the War of 1812, African Americans again helped to win important battles, such as the Battle of New Orleans. In December 1814, General Andrew Jackson was preparing for a major British attack. Needing all the soldiers he could get, Jackson called upon free blacks, promising them "the applause and gratitude of your countrymen."

Jackson formed two African-American battalions headed by white officers. On December 23, he led them in a surprise attack on the British camp. The black soldiers fired their rifles until they ran out of bullets. Then, they used their guns as clubs in fierce hand-to-hand combat. "Soldiers," exclaimed Jackson at the battle's end, "you surpass my hopes."

But after the war, black soldiers did not receive the applause and gratitude that Jackson had promised. Instead, they lost the opportunity to serve their country. By an act of Congress, the peacetime army welcomed only "able-bodied white males."

Although African Americans were forbidden to fight when the Civil War began, they helped the Union Army in other ways. Black men and women served as cooks and nurses. They built bridges and repaired railroads. Some African Americans worked as spies for the Union. By disguising themselves as slaves or as free black workers, they escaped the notice of the Confederates. Harriet Tubman, the well-known abolitionist, often traveled behind enemy lines to locate Confederate camps.

One early hero of the war was an African American serving in the Confederate Navy. Robert Smalls, a slave from South Carolina, was forced into the service of the Confederacy when the Civil War began. Smalls piloted the steamboat *Planter*, which transported guns and supplies.

Harriet Tubman

On May 12, 1862, the *Planter's* white officers spent the night ashore. Quietly, hidden by the darkness, Smalls brought his family on board. He put on the captain's coat and hat. In the early morning hours of May 13, Smalls piloted the *Planter* out of the Charleston harbor to the sea. Smalls turned the vessel and headed north, sailing past Fort Sumter and other Confederate posts. If the Confederates spotted a slave at the wheel, they would shoot, of course, but Union ships posed a danger as well. Their crews would fire upon any Confederate ship.

Robert Smalls

Safely away from Charleston, Smalls raised a white flag to show the Union troops that he wished to surrender the ship. It did not take long for Union sailors to spot the *Planter*. They readied their guns for an attack. Suddenly, one sailor called out, "I see something that looks like a white flag." The Union sailors held their fire.

Smalls turned his ship over to the Union Navy, along with its valuable cargo of weapons, food, and other supplies. "I thought the *Planter* might be of some use to Uncle Abe!" he said, referring to President Lincoln.

At first, the Civil War *was* a white man's war. Whites did most of the fighting—and most of the dying. Across the southern countryside, thousands of soldiers lost their lives.

The first important Civil War battle took place in Virginia, beside a meandering river called Bull Run. The violence of that battle surprised the residents of Washington, D.C. Many had crossed the Potomac River to watch the fight. They planned to eat picnic lunches and enjoy the July day. The strength of the Confederates surprised the young and untrained Union forces, too. They retreated in panic, leaving behind 3,000 soldiers killed, wounded, or captured. Soldiers and sightseers raced back to the safety of the capital. They left the road to Washington littered with guns and picnic baskets.

Routed at Bull Run, the Union Army called for more troops, and people braced themselves for a war that would be anything but quick and easy. No one, however, could have predicted how bloody the conflict would be.

In April 1862, at the Battle of Shiloh, in Tennessee, the Union Army lost 13,000 men. In May 1862, the Union Army suffered 5,000 dead at Seven Pines, Virginia. "Victory has no charms when purchased at such a cost," remarked the Union general George B. McClellan.

The two armies returned to Bull Run in August 1862. This time, 25,000 soldiers, Union and Confederate, were captured, wounded, or killed. Union nurse Clara Barton, who later founded the American Red Cross, reported that the dead and wounded "covered acres."

September 17, 1862, was the bloodiest single day of the war. Near the town of Sharpsburg, Maryland, by Antietam Creek, Union and Confederate soldiers engaged in a series of furious assaults. The battlefield was so bloody that, in the words of one soldier, "the whole landscape for an instant turned

slightly red." Twenty-two thousand soldiers—12,000 Union troops and 10,000 Confederates—were killed or wounded.

A bridge across Antietam Creek, near the famous battlefield

It became clear to the North that this conflict could no longer be a "white man's war." There were not enough white men to meet the need for soldiers. The Union had to call upon African Americans to join the fight.

That summer, Congress had passed the Militia Act of 1862. This act allowed the President to employ blacks "for any military or naval service for which they may be found competent." Two months later, five days after the bloody Battle of Antietam, Lincoln took a much bigger step, a step that changed the course and the very purpose of the war.

On September 22, 1862, Lincoln signed the Emancipation Proclamation. This document declared that the slaves in territories held by the Confederates were to be "forever free," effective January 1, 1863. Of course, Lincoln realized that the southern states would not free their slaves. He also knew that the proclamation did not cover the 800,000 slaves who lived outside the south. But with the Emancipation Proclamation, Lincoln had broadened the nature of the war. The Civil War became more than a struggle to save the Union. It became a war to free the slaves.

The Emancipation Proclamation contained more good news for African Americans. Lincoln had used the power granted to him by the Militia Act of 1862. The Emancipation Proclamation opened the armed forces to blacks, allowing them to serve in "forts, positions, stations, and other places, and to man vessels of all sorts." With the signing of the Emancipation Proclamation, the U.S. Army at last welcomed the many African Americans who wanted to fight.

An elaborately decorated copy of the Emancipation Proclamation, the document that freed the slaves

Chapter 4

Brave and Steady

African Americans rejoiced at the opportunity to serve in uniform. "Once let the black man get upon his person the brass letters 'U.S.,'" wrote Frederick Douglass, "let him get an eagle on his buttons and a musket on his shoulder and bullets in his pocket, and there is no power on earth which can deny that he has earned the right to citizenship in the United States."

While some whites in the north objected to the idea of black soldiers, others welcomed their help. "By arming the Negro we have added a powerful ally," said the Union general Ulysses S. Grant. "They will make good soldiers."

The first five black regiments were formed in South Carolina, Louisiana, and Kansas, during the fall of 1862. Both escaped slaves and free black men enlisted. As in previous wars, African-American soldiers served under white officers.

Within months, African-American recruits were fighting the Confederates. In January 1863, the First South Carolina Volunteers, one of the new black regiments, went on a midnight march through Township, Florida. Suddenly, they came upon a group of Confederate cavalrymen—soldiers on horseback.

The Confederates quickly surrounded the black fighting men, thinking they would be easy to defeat. But the Southerners had made a mistake.

"Nobody knows anything about these men, who has not seen them in battle," remarked the black regiment's commander, Colonel Thomas Wentworth Higginson. "There is a fiery energy about them beyond anything of which I have ever read."

Confederate soldiers used hounds in skirmishes against the First South Carolina Volunteers.

The First South Carolina Volunteers fought off the enemy cavalry, killing twelve of the soldiers, including the Confederate company commander. One black soldier lost his life in the fight.

The South Carolina regiment also conducted raids along southern rivers. They traveled in steamboats, including the *Planter*, the boat that had been commandeered by Robert Smalls. In January 1863, while traveling down the Saint Mary's River, they again met Confederate cavalrymen. "We could see mounted men by the hundred, galloping through the woods, from point to point, to await us," Higginson reported.

The African-American soldiers on deck began loading their guns and firing rapidly. They called to one another, "Never give it up!"

Higginson ordered the men into the ship's hold, the space below the deck, for safety. "When they collected in the hold," he observed, "they actually fought each other for places at the few portholes from which they could fire on the enemy."

While navigating the river, Higginson often turned to Corporal Robert Sutton for advice. Sutton had lived for years as a slave near the Saint Mary's River. Higginson praised Sutton, calling him "the real conductor" of the military expedition. "In every instance when I followed his advice," Higginson said, "the predicted result followed, and I never departed from it, however slightly, without finding reason for subsequent regret."

Black soldiers from the south not only knew the terrain, they had a reason to fight more fiercely than northern soldiers. "Instead of leaving their homes and families to fight, they are fighting for their homes and families," Higginson wrote. "It would have been madness to attempt, with the bravest white troops, what I have successfully accomplished with black ones."

Brigadier General R. Saxton mentioned another good reason to use black soldiers in the south. The sight of former slaves, armed and marching into Florida, he noted, "caused a perfect panic among the rebels throughout the state."

Saxton, too, praised the performance of the First South Carolina Volunteers. "The colored soldiers behaved bravely in all their various actions with the enemy," he reported, "and in no case did they display any inferiority in point of courage to other soldiers."

Black soldiers fought in a major battle that took place at Port Hudson, Louisiana, during May and June of 1863. Two black regiments—the First and Third Louisiana Native Guards—were part of the force that attacked this Confederate post.

A massive fortification protected the town of Port Hudson, located beside the Mississippi River. Its walls were twenty feet thick and surrounded by a fifteen-foot deep, water-filled ditch. Felled trees formed a semicircle at the base of the fort. Their branches had been sharpened to form a treacherous barrier.

The Union needed to seize Port Hudson to gain control of the Mississippi River. This great waterway flowed through the Confederacy and into the Gulf of Mexico. The North hoped to weaken the Confederacy by splitting it in two. And once it controlled the Mississippi, the North would be able to use the river as a shipping route.

General Nathaniel Banks, the Union commander, positioned his forces in the woods around Port Hudson. On the morning of May 27, 1863, the battle began. African Americans had a chance to prove their bravery and fighting skill in a head-on assault against the fort's rugged barricades.

Who were these black fighting men? Some of the men had recently been slaves. Others had lived for years in freedom. Some soldiers were barely more than boys, like sixteen-year-old John Crow-

A young African American was transformed . . .

der, who had lied about his age to join the Army. Others were worldly and educated men, like André Cailloux. Proud of his dark skin, Cailloux called himself "the blackest man in New Orleans."

At 10 AM, the black regiments received the order to advance. Confederate sharpshooters fired at them, yet the Union soldiers marched on. Even when they came under attack from cannons, the soldiers kept moving forward. They came into the open and formed battle lines. Then, with muskets aimed and ready, they charged the enemy's positions.

. . . when he joined the U.S. Colored Troops.

"Valiantly did the heroic descendants of Africa move forward," reported a white lieutenant. The enemy's gunfire grew more intense. Many men fell, wounded or dead.

At last, unable to break through the Confederate barricades, the black regiments retreated. Before the assault was over, they charged five more times. The heavy gunfire "would have confused and almost disorganized the bravest troops," said the lieutenant. "But these men did not swerve, or show cowardice."

One black soldier lost his leg when an artillery shell exploded at his feet. He pulled himself to a log, sat down, and continued shooting. "Never mind me," he told his captain. "Take care of yourself."

Another African American kept fighting with a wounded leg. "They want me to go to the hospital," he said, "but I guess I can give 'em a little more yet."

André Cailloux fought on after a bullet shattered his arm. Then, a second bullet hit him, and he fell. John Crowder, the patriotic teenager, also died in the battle.

African Americans fought bravely in the assault on Port Hudson.

Everyone who saw the combat performance of the First and Third Louisiana Native Guards was impressed. "You have no idea how my prejudices with regard to negro troops have been dispelled," said one white officer. "The brigade of negroes behaved magnificently and fought splendidly; [they] could not have done better." The *New York Times* proclaimed, "It is no longer possible to doubt the bravery and steadiness of the colored race."

Within weeks, another regiment would win the black soldiers even greater glory.

"It is no longer possible to doubt the bravery and steadiness of the colored race."

Chapter 5

Forward, 54th!

In January 1863, as African-American soldiers fought in Florida, a new black regiment took shape in Massachusetts. Known as the 54th Massachusetts Volunteer Infantry, it would become the best-known black fighting unit of the Civil War.

Recruiting posters went up in cities and towns across the north. "Men of Color! To Arms!" they read. The posters promised black soldiers the same pay and treatment that white soldiers received. Volunteers came from all over New England. They came from New York, Pennsylvania, the Midwest, and even Canada.

Charles Douglass enlisted, along with his brother Lewis. The two were sons of Frederick Douglass. William Carney signed up. He hoped one day to be a minister. A whaler from New Bedford, Massachusetts, James Henry Gooding,

COME AND JOIN US BROTHERS.

also volunteered. A man who loved to read and write poetry, Gooding wrote letters to his hometown newspaper, the *New Bedford Mercury*, describing the regiment's activities.

A recruiting poster from the Philadelphia, Pennsylvania, area

45

Colonel Robert Gould Shaw, the son of a wealthy abolitionist, commanded the black regiment. Shaw believed strongly in equal treatment for African Americans, and he was ready to share equally in any hardships or dangers that his regiment faced.

Colonel Robert
Gould Shaw

The new recruits trained at Camp Meade, Massachusetts. There, they learned to use their weapons and march in formation. Many of Boston's whites traveled to Camp Meade to see the unusual sight of black men performing military drills.

With so many eyes watching them, the soldiers worked hard to do their best. They knew that some people were waiting for them to make mistakes. "*Our* people must consider that their position is a very delicate one," wrote James Henry Gooding. "The least false step, at a moment like the present, may tell a dismal tale at some future day."

In May 1863, with their training completed, the soldiers of the 54th set sail for the coastal islands of South Carolina. "Remember, if I die, I die in a good cause," wrote Lewis Douglass to his fiancée.

One new soldier wrote a song that expressed his regiment's patriotism and fighting spirit:

So rally, boys, rally,
let us never mind the past;
We had a hard road to travel,
but our day is coming fast,
For God is for the right,
and we have no need to fear,—

"Remember, if I die, I die in a good cause."

47

The Union must be saved
by the colored volunteer.

In South Carolina, the soldiers discovered a climate and wildlife far different from those of the north. "If a person were to ask me what I saw South," noted Gooding, "I should tell him stink weed, sand, rattlesnakes, and alligators." The 54th Infantry set up camp in these strange new surroundings.

On June 30, when the soldiers were to be paid, they received some distressing news. They learned that they would not be paid at the same rate as white soldiers. While white soldiers received $13.00 per month, plus $3.50 to buy clothing, the black soldiers were to get $10.00 per month, with $3.00 deducted to pay for their uniforms.

Angry, the men of the 54th refused to accept their money. They preferred to serve without pay than to take less than they were due. Turning down their salary meant hardship not only for the men, but for their families as well. Still, the soldiers would accept only what they had earned.

One soldier said, "The ten dollars by the greatest government in the world is an unjust distinction to men who have only black skin to merit it."

Gooding sent a letter to President Lincoln. "We have done a soldier's duty," he wrote. "Why can't we have a soldier's pay?"

African-American soldiers on guard duty

On July 18, 1863, six hundred men of the 54th Infantry entered combat. They were on Morris Island, a sandbar near Fort Sumter. They had marched all night through heavy rain, and they were tired and hungry. But they had no time to sleep or eat. General George C. Strong had asked the 54th Infantry to lead the attack on Fort Wagner.

Fort Wagner was a structure built of sand and sticks, protected by a deep moat. From the top of its walls, Confederate cannons pointed in all directions. The Union leaders wanted to occupy the city of Charleston. Once their forces captured Fort Wagner, they could move in on Fort Sumter and open up the harbor to Union ships.

The attack was to begin at twilight. Before they faced enemy gunfire, Colonel Shaw said a few words to his men. "He sat on the ground and was talking to the men very familiarly and kindly," James Gooding remembered. "He told them how the eyes of thousands would look upon the night's work they were about to do."

Then, Shaw led the soldiers of the 54th Infantry across the half mile of sand that separated them from Fort Wagner. When they were within two hundred feet of the fort, the Confederates opened fire. Shaw shouted, "Forward, 54th!" But

The 54th Infantry's finest hour, storming Fort Wagner

when the men were sixty feet from the fort, the flying bullets forced them to retreat.

Later that evening, the 54th led a second assault on Fort Wagner. This time, Shaw and some of his men reached the top of one of the parapets, the walls that protected the fort. Shaw stood on the wall shouting, "Rally! Rally!" Soon, he was shot and fell dead.

"I saw his face," one survivor recalled. "It was white as snow, but in every line was that courage which led his men to the very crest of that wall of death."

Gooding also witnessed Shaw's death. "When the men saw their gallant leader fall, they made a desperate effort to get him out," he informed the people of New Bedford. Some who tried to reach Shaw were hit by bullets themselves. Others stumbled and fell as they crossed the moat.

Many others also died from Confederate gunfire. "They mowed us down like grass," one soldier said. Some of the 54th's soldiers were killed by "friendly fire." When Union forces at the rear of the attack panicked, they began to shoot their guns wildly, often hitting their own soldiers who were climbing the parapet.

A number of observers described the violence

and confusion of that historic night. "The enemy could be distinguished from our own men only by the light of bursting shell," wrote a newspaper reporter. "The darkness was so intense, the roar of artillery was so loud, the flight of grape [a cluster of iron balls] and canister shot so rapid and destructive that it was absolutely impossible to preserve order."

Abraham F. Brown, a member of the 54th Massachusetts Volunteer Infantry

"I had my sword sheath blown away while on the parapet of the fort," Lewis Douglass wrote. "Swept down like chaff, still our men went on and on."

To James Gooding, the flying ammunition looked like angry, bloodthirsty insects. "The shell and shot come screaming through the air, as though thirsting for a victim," he wrote. "They explode, scattering the fragments around, like a shoal of maddened wasps."

The abolitionist Harriet Tubman served as a nurse for the Union soldiers. She compared the battle to a rainstorm. "We saw the lightning, and that was the guns," Tubman said. "And then we heard the thunder, and that was the big guns; and then we heard the rain falling, and that was the drops of blood falling; and when we came to get in the crops, it was dead men we reaped."

Clara Barton was another nurse at the battle site. She, too, recalled the wounded and the dead. "I can see again the scarlet flow of blood as it rolled over the black limbs beneath my hands, and the great heave of the human heart before it grew still," Barton wrote.

It was a battle that turned young Americans into heroes. One hero at Fort Wagner was Sergeant

William Carney, the twenty-three-year-old soldier who wanted to be a minister. Carney saw a bullet hit his regiment's color bearer, the soldier who carried the American flag. Quickly, Carney reached for the flag and carried it to the front of the attack. There, he held the flag high, giving courage to his comrades, although bullets hit him in the head, chest, arm, and thigh. At last, the order came to retreat. Carney crawled back, using one knee and one hand, still holding up the flag. Later, in a field hospital, he told the other wounded men, "Boys, the old flag never touched the ground."

The Union lost the Battle of Fort Wagner in spite of the 54th Infantry's bravery. But African Americans had once more shown their willingness and ability to fight. The *New York Herald* declared that the 54th Infantry fought "as none but splendid soldiers, splendidly officered, could fight."

The Confederates buried Colonel Shaw with the dead of his regiment. To the men of the South, burial among blacks was an insult. Shaw's family, however, considered his burial site an honor. "We can imagine no holier place than that in which he is, nor wish him better company," wrote Shaw's father. "What a bodyguard he has!"

Sergeant Carney's wounds healed. He became

"Boys, the old flag never touched the ground."

the first African-American soldier to earn the Congressional Medal of Honor, awarded for bravery in action. The exact number of black Medal of Honor winners in the Civil War is uncertain. Some sources claim that there were seventeen, while others have counted as many as twenty-three.

Sergeant William
Carney

Lewis Douglass also survived. "How I got out of that fight I cannot tell, but I am here," he informed his fiancée. "I wish we had 100,000 colored troops. We would put an end to this war."

In January 1864, James Gooding was wounded in a battle in Florida and captured by the Confederates. They brought him to Andersonville Prison in southwest Georgia, known as a place of horror and death. At Andersonville, the Confederates crowded more than 30,000 Union prisoners into an area of about twenty-six acres. The Union men slept on the ground and had almost nothing to eat. They had no clean water to drink. Gooding was one of the 13,000 men who died at Andersonville of starvation, disease, or exposure to the weather.

Gooding did not live to see the 54th Infantry win one of its greatest victories. It was a victory that took place off the battlefield. In August 1864, eighteen months after they had refused unequal pay, the men of the 54th accepted their first payment from the government. It was equal to that which white soldiers received. Their protests and their performance had forced Congress to admit the equality of white and black soldiers.

The 54th's struggle against racial prejudice resulted in a victory for both African Americans and the Union cause. The regiment's reputation for courage convinced a doubting nation that African-American fighting men were a valuable resource. Based on the combat performance of the 54th, the Union Army continued to rely on the service of African Americans. "It is not too much to say that if this Massachusetts 54th had faltered when its time came," wrote the *New York Tribune*, "two hundred thousand troops for whom it was a pioneer would never have been put in the field."

Chapter 6

A Powerful Force

Civil War soldiers, black and white, needed courage in battle and strength in daily life. Between battles, soldiers faced a dreary and draining routine of marching and waiting, marching and waiting. They lived on rations of beans, bacon, dried meat, coffee, and flat, dry biscuits called hardtack.

Soldiers faced the risk of death in battle, of course, but they faced a greater risk of death from disease. Impure food and water and unsanitary conditions led to outbreaks of typhoid, diphtheria, and diarrhea. Crowding allowed such contagious diseases as measles and mumps to spread rapidly. One of every thirteen soldiers died from disease. (Only one of sixty-five died in combat.)

Among African Americans, the death rate from disease was even higher. When they were paid less than white soldiers and could not afford warm clothing, they suffered from exposure to the cold weather. And, at times, white physicians refused to treat black soldiers.

Black soldiers faced other hardships because of their race. If captured, they could expect harsh treatment. The Southerners forced some captured black soldiers to work for the Confederacy. They sold others as slaves. They tortured or killed many more, as an example to other blacks. The Southern forces wanted to frighten African Americans out of fighting for the Union.

One of the worst instances of Southern cruelty to black soldiers is known as the Fort Pillow Massacre. The Union post Fort Pillow stood beside the Mississippi River in Tennessee. Stationed there were 570 Union soldiers, white and black. On April 12, 1864, the Confederates captured the fort. They murdered many black soldiers who tried to surrender. Some they shot; others they burned alive.

A Confederate soldier recalled the slaughter: "The poor, deluded Negroes would run up to our men, fall upon their knees with uplifted hands, scream for mercy, but were ordered to their feet and shot down."

The Confederate general Nathan Bedford Forrest coldly explained the South's purpose. "It is hoped," he said, "that these facts will demonstrate to the Northern people that negro soldiers cannot cope with southerners."

After the Fort Pillow Massacre, African-American troops fought more fiercely than ever before. "Remember Fort Pillow!" became their battle cry.

At Petersburg, Virginia, black soldiers again learned the high cost of their courage. The Union

African-American soldiers were massacred at Fort Pillow, Tennessee.

general Ambrose Burnside had the idea to dig a five hundred-foot tunnel under the Confederate fort at Petersburg and fill it with gunpowder. Burnside wanted to blast a hole in Petersburg's defenses and take the town.

At dawn, on July 30, 1864, the fuse was lit. The gunpowder exploded. "Suddenly, the earth trembled beneath our feet," a Union general reported. A mushroom-shaped cloud of fire and dirt rose into the sky. When the air cleared, the soldiers saw a huge crater 30 feet deep, 60 feet wide, and 170 feet long.

Burnside ordered the Union forces to charge. Three white regiments went forward, and a black regiment followed closely. They moved down into the crater and realized—too late—that they had made a mistake. The sides of the pit were too steep for the soldiers to climb out.

The Confederates allowed many white soldiers to surrender, but any blacks who gave themselves up were killed. "The whole floor of the trench was strewn with the dead bodies of negroes," a Confederate soldier observed.

Despite losses such as those at Fort Pillow and Petersburg, the enthusiasm and energy of the Union's black soldiers made them a strong and powerful fighting force. As the months passed, the number of black soldiers grew. By October 1864, there were 140 black regiments. Lincoln realized that the "physical force" of the African-American troops was helping to win the war. "Keep it and you can save the Union," the President said. "Throw it away and the Union goes with it."

Black soldiers fought in nearly every battle in the last year of the war. In September 1864, black regiments stormed the Confederate fortifications at New Market Heights, Virginia. On the same day, other black regiments fought a bloody battle at nearby Chaffin's Farm. The fight was so brutal that the 4th and 6th United States Colored Troops lost half their men. After almost every officer in the 5th was wounded, four black sergeants took command of the regiment. These men were awarded Congressional Medals of Honor.

In the Battle of Nashville, Tennessee, in December 1864, eight black regiments took part in an attack on the Confederate Army. "Colored soldiers had again fought side by side with white troops," observed Colonel Thomas J. Morgan of the 14th United States Colored Infantry. "They had mingled together in the charge; they had supported each other; they had assisted each other from the field when wounded; and they lay side by side in death . . . . The survivors rejoiced together over a hard-fought field, won by a common valor."

After seeing the Union's success with African-American troops, some Confederates began to ask why they, too, did not employ black soldiers. The South badly needed a source of military manpower. By 1864, many of its white troops had been killed or wounded. As the list of Union victories kept mounting, arming the slaves seemed the only possible way for the South to continue the war. As Judah P. Benjamin, the Confederate secretary of war, explained, "The negroes will certainly be made to fight against us if not armed for our defense."

On March 13, 1865, the Confederate president, Jefferson Davis, signed the Negro Soldier Law, which called for the training of 300,000 black soldiers. But before the training could begin, the Union captured Richmond, Virginia, the Confederate capital. The war was nearly at an end.

A month later, it was over. On April 9, 1865, at Appomattox Courthouse, Virginia, Robert E. Lee, the commanding general of the Confederate forces, surrendered to Union general Ulysses S. Grant.

More than 200,000 African Americans served in the U.S. armed forces during the Civil War. They made up nearly one-tenth of the Union troops. The war had claimed the lives of 620,000 Americans, including 38,000 blacks.

With the war over, the surviving soldiers were eager to turn in their weapons and head home. "I want to go home so bad," wrote one black soldier. "It seems to me that I have been gone from home 70 years and longer."

Homecoming for African-American soldiers at Little Rock, Arkansas, 1866

The Union soldiers traveled back to the cities where they had enlisted. There, they received their discharge papers and their final Army pay. Soldiers and officers bid their good byes. "Go now, black soldiers, to your houses," said Lieutenant Colonel James Brisbin of the 6th U.S. Colored Cavalry. "The flag that now floats over us is as much yours, as it is mine."

Chapter 7

Patience and Patriotism

During the Civil War, an African-American soldier from Rhode Island expressed this goal for his people and his country. "This will yet be a pleasant land for the colored man to dwell in," wrote James F. Jones in 1864. "Step by step we are emerging from darkness into light."

African Americans fought and died in the Civil War for a number of reasons: to save the Union, to secure their rights, and to free the slaves. At the same time, they fought for equality within the armed forces. The struggle continued in the years ahead.

Following the Civil War, the U.S. government guaranteed African Americans the rights promised by the Constitution to the "People of the United States." The nation's leaders passed three historic amendments, or additions, to the Constitution.

Nathan Bedford
Forrest

The Thirteenth Amendment outlawed slavery in the United States. The Fourteenth Amendment made the former slaves citizens of the United States. It also declared that no state could "deprive any person of life, liberty, or property without due process of law." This amendment protected African Americans from unfair punishments and attacks. The Fifteenth Amendment, passed in 1870, guaranteed blacks the right to vote. The government passed these amendments to insure equal treatment under the law for all Americans, but the struggle for racial equality was far from over.

Once southerners could no longer own slaves, they took measures to prevent African Americans from gaining political or economic power. The southern states passed laws called "Black Codes," which strictly limited blacks' freedom. Other laws, known as "Jim Crow" laws, created a system of racial segregation. These laws required separate public facilities for blacks and whites—from separate schools to separate railroad cars, from separate rest rooms to separate drinking fountains. The Supreme Court ruled in 1896 that this form of segregation was legal, as long as the facilities were equal. However, southern communities always provided better services for whites than for blacks.

Some southerners formed hate groups based on a belief in white superiority. The best known and most feared was the Ku Klux Klan. It was organized by Nathan Forrest, the Confederate general who ordered the murder of African-American prisoners during the Civil War. Wearing white robes and hoods, Klan members used threats and violence to frighten southern blacks.

To escape unfair treatment, and to find jobs, black people began a "Great Migration" to northern states. The black population of northern cities grew dramatically in the early twentieth century. For example, 12,000 African Americans lived in New York City in 1860. By 1900, that number had reached 60,000. And, by 1910, it had passed 91,000. In the cities of the north, conditions for African Americans were somewhat better. Segregated schools had been outlawed in many places. Some northern states had also passed laws forbidding the segregation of public facilities by race.

Few blacks, however, felt welcome in the north. White workers, afraid that black men and women would take their jobs, refused to let them join labor unions. White northerners often denied housing and services to African Americans.

Many African Americans looked to the opportunity offered by the military. In 1866, African Americans had at last gained the right to serve during peacetime. The Army formed four black regiments—the 9th and 10th Cavalry, and the 24th and 25th Infantry. These men, known as the Buffalo Soldiers, helped to settle the western frontier. They served during the Indian Wars, a tragic episode in American history. As the United States expanded west, it seized land from the Native Americans and destroyed their way of life. The Buffalo Soldiers helped to keep peace between Indians and settlers.

In 1898, the Buffalo Soldiers became the first African Americans to battle on foreign soil. They fought with bravery and distinction in Cuba during the Spanish-American War. At times, they came to the aid of less-experienced white forces. "They didn't seem to know what fear was," observed a white soldier.

In 1917, the United States entered World War I. Most of the 140,000 African Americans who served in this war against Germany did not fight the enemy. They performed such jobs as driving trucks, repairing vehicles, and unloading ships. But 40,000 blacks went into combat, and the Army trained nearly 700 black officers to serve with black regiments. Army leaders would not allow an African American to command white troops.

The nation gained its first black general, Benjamin O. Davis, Sr., in 1940. In the following year, the United States entered World War II. More than a million African Americans served in this war. Colonel Benjamin O. Davis, Jr., the general's son, commanded the first African-American combat pilots, the Tuskegee Airmen.

The performance of African Americans in World War II convinced President Harry S Truman to end segregation in the U.S. armed forces in 1948. When Americans went to war again, in 1950, black and white soldiers served together in integrated units. Along with the forces of fifteen other countries, these Americans helped South Korea fight off an invasion from North Korea and China.

In the 1960s and 1970s, the United States fought another war in Asia, in the small nation of Vietnam. Blacks made up only 11 percent of the U.S. population, but they accounted for 23 percent of combat deaths in Vietnam. Despite the risks that they faced, African Americans showed a high level of courage. One out of every five Congressional Medals of Honor awarded for service in Vietnam went to an African American.

African Americans have continued to make gains in the armed forces. In 1989, President George Bush appointed a black officer to the highest military position in the nation. General Colin Powell became the first African-American chairman of the Joint Chiefs of Staff. Under Powell's direction, the American armed forces won a swift victory in the Persian Gulf War of 1991. Troops from the United States and other nations defeated the army of Iraq, which had invaded its neighbor Kuwait.

Although the struggle continues, black soldiers have indeed made important gains since the day the first African-American regiment to fight in the Civil War was disbanded.

On that day in February 1866, the First South Carolina Volunteers were camped at Morris Island, where the 54th Infantry had fought so valiantly. Lieutenant Colonel C. T. Trowbridge delivered a farewell address to the regiment. His words honor all of the African-American soldiers who fought for their country during the Civil War:

> *It seems fitting to me that the last hours of our existence as a regiment should be passed amidst the unmarked graves of your com-*

rades—at Fort Wagner. Near you rest the bones of Colonel Shaw, buried by an enemy's hand, in the same grave with his black soldiers, who fell at his side; where, in future, your children's children will come on pilgrimages to do homage to the ashes of those that fell in this glorious struggle . . . .

Your toils are ended, your mission is fulfilled, and we separate forever. The fidelity, patience, and patriotism with which you have discharged your duties, to your men and to your country, entitle you to a far higher tribute than any words of thankfulness which I can give you from the bottom of my heart. You will find your reward in the proud conviction that the cause for which you have battled so nobly has been crowned with abundant success.

Americans continue to pay tribute to the black soldiers who fought in the Civil War. Visitors to Boston Common, in Massachusetts, may stop to see a large stone memorial to the 54th Massachusetts Volunteer Infantry. Created by the American sculptor Augustus Saint-Gaudens, and dedicated in 1897, the memorial shows members of the historic regiment marching toward battle, their rifles held against their shoulders. Since 1989, millions of people have learned the story of the 54th from the Academy Award-winning motion picture "Glory."

Every year, four million people visit Arlington National Cemetery, on the banks of the Potomac River near Washington, D.C. Many who stroll along the paths of this great military cemetery pass a young tree, an American red maple. This tree was planted in 1991 as a living memorial to all African Americans who served in the Civil War as soldiers, sailors, or civilians. It honors the black Civil War heroes buried at Arlington, as well as those whose graves are scattered across the north and south.

A plaque beside the tree thanks these dead heroes on behalf of the generations of African Americans who have benefited from their sacrifices. "Lest we forget," the inscription reads, "we stand on your shoulders."

The 54th Massachusetts Volunteer Infantry Memorial, Boston, Massachusetts

74

Chronology

African Americans in the U.S. Armed Forces

1770	On March 5, Crispus Attucks, a former slave, is among the first to die in the "Boston Massacre."
1776-1781	7,000 African-American soldiers and sailors take part in the Revolutionary War.
1776	On January 16, the Continental Congress agrees to enlist free blacks.
1812-1815	Black soldiers and sailors fight against the British troops at such critical battles as Lake Erie and New Orleans.
1862-1865	186,000 African-American soldiers serve in black regiments during the Civil War; 38,000 black soldiers lose their lives in more than 400 battles.
1862	On July 17, the U.S. Congress approves the enlistment of black soldiers.
1865	On March 13, the Confederate States of America begins to accept black recruits.
1866-1890	Units of black soldiers, referred to as Buffalo Soldiers, are formed as part of the U.S. Army.
1872	On September 21, John H. Conyers becomes the first African American admitted to the U.S. Naval Academy.
1877	On June 15, Henry O. Flipper becomes the first African American to graduate from West Point.
1914-1918	More than 400,000 African Americans serve in the U.S. armed forces during the First World War.

On May 15, two black soldiers, Henry Johnson and Needham Roberts become the first Americans to receive the French Medal of Honor *(Croix de Guerre).*	1918
In June, Benjamin O. Davis, Jr., graduates from West Point, the first black American to do so in the twentieth century.	1936
Benjamin O. Davis, Sr., becomes the first African-American general in the active Regular Army.	1940
American forces in World War II include more than a million African-American men and women.	1941-1945
On March 25, the Army Air Corps forms its first black unit, the 99th Pursuit Squadron.	1941
On August 24, Colonel Benjamin O. Davis, Jr., is made commander of the 99th Pursuit Squadron.	1942
On January 27 and 28, the airmen of the 99th Pursuit Squadron score a major victory against enemy fighters at the Italian seaside town of Anzio.	1944
On February 2, President Harry S Truman signs Executive Order 9981, ordering an end to segregation in the U.S. armed forces.	1948
Black and white forces fight side by side in Korea as separate black fighting units are disbanded.	1950-1953
Twenty African-American soldiers are awarded the Congressional Medal of Honor during the Vietnam War.	1965-1973
On April 28, Samuel L. Gravely becomes the first black admiral in the history of the U.S. Navy.	1971
In August, Daniel "Chappie" James becomes the first African American to achieve the rank of four-star general.	1975
On October 3, Colin Powell becomes the first African-American chairman of the Joint Chiefs of Staff.	1989
100,000 African-American men and women are sent to the Middle East during the Persian Gulf conflict.	1990-1991
On July 25, the Buffalo Soldier Monument is dedicated at Fort Leavenworth, Kansas.	1992

Index

Bibliography

Berlin, Ira, ed. *Freedom: A Documentary History of Emancipation 1861-1867* (Series II: The Black Military Experience). Cambridge, UK: Cambridge University Press, 1982.

Foote, Shelby. *The Civil War: A Narrative, Vol. II, Fredericksburg to Meridian.* New York: Vintage Books, 1963.

Franklin, John Hope. *From Slavery to Freedom: A History of Negro Americans* (Fifth Edition). New York: Alfred A. Knopf, 1980.

Glatthaar, Joseph T. *Forged in Battle: The Civil War Alliance of Black Soldiers and White Officers.* New York: The Free Press, 1990.

Gooding, Corporal James Henry. *On the Altar of Freedom: A Black Soldier's Civil War Letters from the Front.* Amherst, MA: The University of Massachusetts Press, 1991.

Greene, Robert Ewell. *Black Defenders of America: 1775-1973.* Chicago: Johnson Publishing, 1974.

McPherson, James M. *The Negro's Civil War: How American Blacks Felt and Acted During the War for the Union.* New York: Ballantine Books, 1991.

Quarles, Benjamin. *The Negro in the Civil War.* New York: Da Capo Press, 1953.

Wakin, Edward. *Black Fighting Men in U.S. History.* New York: Lothrop, Lee & Shepard, 1971.

Ward, Geoffrey C., with Rick Burns and Ken Burns. *The Civil War.* New York: Alfred A. Knopf, 1990.

"The Massachusetts Colored Infantry." Episode of the PBS television series "The American Experience."

DEMCO